A TRUE BOOK

W9-BBC-567

The Ute

DISCARD

KEVIN CUNNINGHAM
AND PETER BENOIT

Children's Press®
An Imprint of Scholastic Inc.
New York   Toronto   London   Auckland   Sydney
Mexico City   New Delhi   Hong Kong
Danbury, Connecticut

Content Consultant

Scott Manning Stevens, PhD
Director, McNickle Center
Newberry Library
Chicago, Illinois

Library of Congress Cataloging-in-Publication Data

Cunningham, Kevin, 1966–
  The Ute/by Kevin Cunningham and Peter Benoit.
     p. cm. — (A true book)
  Includes bibliographical references and index.
  ISBN-13: 978-0-531-20765-9 (lib. bdg.)   978-0-531-29307-2 (pbk.)
  ISBN-10: 0-531-20765-X (lib. bdg.)   0-531-29307-6 (pbk.)
  1. Ute Indians—Juvenile literature. 2. Ute Indians—History—Juvenile literature. 3. Southwest,
New—History—Juvenile literature. I. Benoit, Peter, 1955– II. Title. III. Series.
  E99.U8C86 2011
  979.004'974576—dc22   2010051578

All rights reserved. Published in 2011 by Children's Press, an imprint of Scholastic Inc.
Printed in China 62
SCHOLASTIC, CHILDREN'S PRESS, A TRUE BOOK and associated logos are trademarks and/or registered trademarks of Scholastic Inc.

1 2 3 4 5 6 7 8 9 10 R 19 18 17 16 15 14 13 12 11

Find the Truth!

Everything you are about to read is true *except* for one of the sentences on this page.

Which one is **TRUE**?

T or F The Ute never rode on horseback.

T or F Ute dance the Bear Dance to honor the grizzly.

Find the answers in this book.

Contents

**Beaded moccasins
and leggings**

THE BIG TRUTH!

The Yearly Migration

Pine nuts were an important source of protein for the Ute during the winter. ➡

3 Ceremonies

4 Coming Back

**Ute women
and children**

5

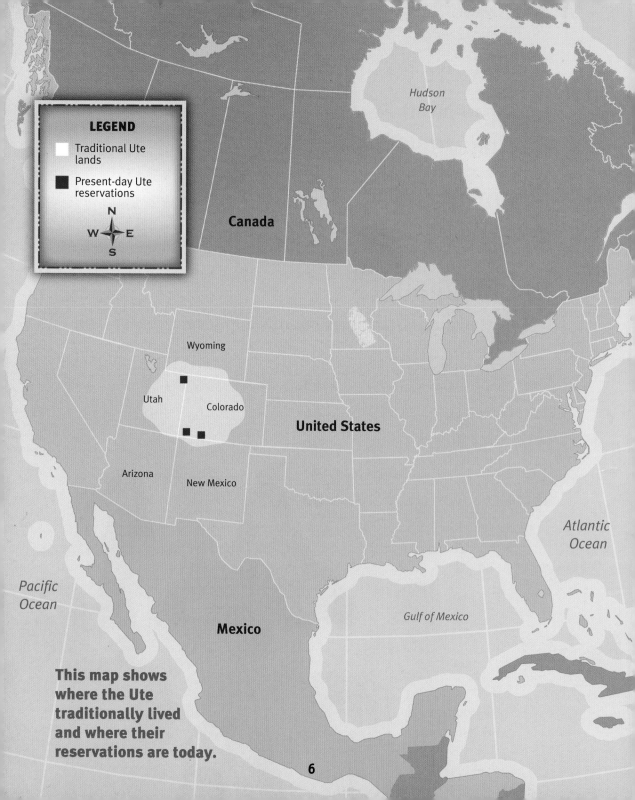

LEGEND

Traditional Ute lands

Present-day Ute reservations

N W E S

Canada

Hudson Bay

United States

Wyoming

Utah

Colorado

Arizona

New Mexico

Mexico

Pacific Ocean

Gulf of Mexico

Atlantic Ocean

This map shows where the Ute traditionally lived and where their reservations are today.

CHAPTER 1

Living Off the Land

The Ute people say they have lived on their land in the Rocky Mountain regions of present-day Colorado and Utah since the beginning of time. Many experts in **archaeology**, however, think the Ute's ancestors once lived in southwestern Nevada. Between 1300 and 1500 C.E., the experts say, the Ute **migrated** to their present lands. The name Ute comes from *Yuta*, the name given them by the Spanish. The Ute called themselves *Nuutsiu* or *Nuche*, meaning "the people."

← The state of Utah is named after the Ute.

On the Move

The Ute gathered into bands, or groups, made up of several related families. A band migrated from one location to another during the year. In general, they returned each year to well-known places that offered useful wild plants and reliable hunting or fishing. Foods available in one place in summer differed from those found somewhere else in the fall. Since a band migrated hundreds of miles through many landscapes, Utes usually enjoyed a variety of foods.

The Ute used gathering baskets to collect berries and other foods.

Rose hips contain as much as 40 times more vitamin C than oranges.

Rose hips are the fruits of rosebushes. They are roughly the size of cherries.

Plants in the Diet

The Ute harvested huge numbers of wild plants. Rose hips and berries, including strawberries and elderberries, were eaten raw, or they were dried and used later in stews. Sunflower seeds were another favorite. Acorns and many other nuts were also gathered. Ute women used strong sticks to dig up wild onions as well as the roots of wild potatoes and the yampa, a wild carrot sometimes called an Indian carrot. In the spring, aspen trees provided sap for food.

Pine Nut Feast

Though an important food, pine nuts were not easy to come by. Pinyon pines that shed the nuts only grow on mountainsides above 5,500 feet (1,700 meters). Freezing air causes cones on the trees to fall. Ute women struck the cracked cones to take out the nuts. Later, they roasted the pine nuts and ground them into flour for cakes or stews.

Pine nuts were a staple of the Ute diet. Although they are called nuts, they are actually seeds.

Ute Homes

Utes built several kinds of shelters. On the western side of the Rockies, Utes put up huts with grass roofs. The dome-shaped **wickiup** was another common structure. Utes started a wickiup by driving four wooden poles into the ground. After tying the poles together, the builders covered the wooden frame with bark, grass, and brush. Willow branches held the plant material in place.

The inside of a Ute wickiup stayed cool during hot summers.

Some Ute moccasins were decorated with beadwork in floral designs.

Ute moccasins and leggings

Buckskin, Bags, and Breechcloths

The Ute preferred clothes made from the softened hides of deer (called buckskin), mountain sheep, and antelope.

Ute women favored dresses made from two skins of does (female deer) attached at the shoulders and sides. Bags for personal items hung from a belt. Ute women wore leggings sewn to **moccasins**, a deerskin or elk-skin shoe like a slipper. They parted their hair in the middle.

Ute men wore buckskin shirts decorated with fringe and animal hair. **Breechcloths** were long, rectangular buckskin pieces that covered them below the waist in the front and back. They also wore leggings. Like women, they walked in moccasins, except in the desert, when both men and women made sandals or went barefoot. Ute men kept their hair in two braids and sometimes tied fur into a braid.

After they got horses, the Ute hunted bison (buffalo) and used the hides for clothing.

Ute men and women often wore necklaces made from seeds, stones, or animal bones.

The Spanish brought hundreds of horses to New Mexico. The Ute were using the animals by the mid-1600s.

CHAPTER 2

The Invaders

From the 1540s on, Spanish explorers and settlers wound their way into what is today the southwestern United States. A 1637 battle between Utes and Spaniards resulted in Ute prisoners being sent to the Spanish city of Santa Fe, New Mexico. Three years later, some of the prisoners escaped. As they did, they stole some Spanish horses. Soon horses would change the Ute forever.

The Ute may have been the first Native Americans in North America to acquire horses.

There were no horses in the Americas when Christopher Columbus landed in 1492. After 1493, however, Spanish settlers brought European animals with them. The Ute, like many Native American peoples, quickly saw how useful horses could be. After 1640, the Ute journeyed often to the Southwest to trade for them. They captured more in raids on Spanish settlements.

The Ute were skilled riders. Here, a Ute man and woman pose on horseback.

Some Ute warriors owned as many as a dozen horses.

Some Ute teepees were 17 feet (5 m) high.

More Changes

With horses to ride, the Ute living east of the Rockies left the mountains and migrated as far as the Great Plains. They began to use teepees, which were common among Plains peoples. These homes fit their new **mobile** lifestyle because a horse could carry the teepee pieces, and just a few people could put one together. The Eastern Ute met with new native peoples for trade and to exchange ideas—and, sometimes, to raid their villages and fight them.

Horses made it easier for the Ute to react to attacks and defend themselves from their enemies.

New Ways, New Threats

By the 1800s, the Ute had a reputation as excellent raiders. They now used iron and steel bought from the Spaniards and kept herds of horses. The Ute had both fought the Spanish and helped them in battles with the powerful Comanche. But soon a new threat appeared. The 1820s saw more and more whites crossing Ute lands. These were no longer Spaniards, but Americans headed west.

The Black Hawk War of 1865-1867

On the other side of the Rockies, the Western Ute bumped against Mormon settlers streaming into the Utah region. Utes became frustrated as the Mormons kept them from their usual hunting, fishing, and herding areas. Mormons, on the other hand, were angry about Ute raids. The Mormon leader Brigham Young told his people to "feed them, not fight them." But the bad feelings led to the Black Hawk War of 1865–1867.

Young established more than 300 Mormon settlements in the United States, Mexico, and Canada.

Brigham Young

The Ute and their Indian allies gathered under a leader named Black Hawk. For two years, they fought quick battles with the Mormons and raided settlements. About 50 Mormons and more than 50 Ute died before Black Hawk, wounded and sick, all but ended the war

Although Black Hawk's men occasionally killed settlers, more often they stole Mormons' cattle.

by leaving the fight. By then, however, the weakened Utes had already begun moving to a **reservation**—land set aside for them that was controlled by the U.S. government.

The Colorado Ute

In Colorado, an 1863 **treaty** had promised the Ute the western side of the San Juan Mountains. In 1868, however, whites wanted the land and the gold that they believed was there. They insisted the government move the Ute to small reservations. The Ute chief Ouray managed to hold out for a treaty that promised a larger reservation and money. Soon white leaders started a **campaign** to remove the Ute from the entire Colorado Territory.

Ouray spoke four languages, including English and Spanish.

Ouray traveled to Washington, D.C., several times in efforts to obtain fair treaties for the Ute.

Farming and Hunting

In 1878, Nathan C. Meeker became the U.S. government agent at the Ute White River Reservation. Meeker viewed the Ute as children and savages. His mission, he believed, was to make them behave in the way he thought proper, by teaching them to farm. Though some Ute tried growing crops, most preferred their old ways. In the summer, they mounted horses as usual and deserted the fields to hunt.

Meeker had once worked as a reporter in New York.

Nathan C. Meeker tried to force the Ute to farm by withholding government shipments of supplies and food.

Government agents pressured the Ute into raising crops such as turnips.

Meeker's Mistakes

Meeker angered the Ute when he plowed land they had used as a popular racetrack. Worse, he insulted the Ute in official reports and newspaper articles. A **drought** in 1879 sparked forest fires and turned the Ute against farming. But Meeker persisted. He even took more Ute land for farming. The Ute became angrier when Meeker said that the land belonged to the government instead of them.

In the 1879 conflict at White River, the Ute took Meeker's daughter, wife, and others captive. They were eventually released.

Violence at White River

On September 29, 1879, Ute warriors attacked U.S. soldiers sent to keep peace. For six days, the Ute kept the soldiers trapped inside a circle of wagons and dead horses. More soldiers arrived on October 5. But the battle ended suddenly when a group of chiefs led by Ouray ordered the Ute to stop. Nearby, however, the Ute had killed Meeker and 10 others. Furious Coloradans demanded that all the Ute be sent away.

March to the Reservation

Ouray traveled to Washington, D.C., to work out a peace plan with the U.S. government. But he had little power to resist what the government wanted. In August 1881, army troops marched the Ute out of Colorado. Many ended up on the Ute Reservation in Utah, farming unwanted, empty land. Behind them, white settlers rushed in to claim the mountains the Ute had wandered over for 500 years.

The name *Chipeta* means "white singing bird."

Ouray and his wife, Chipeta, pose for a photograph. Chipeta, like Ouray, worked hard to achieve peace between the Ute and government officials.

25

The Yearly Migration

A Ute band migrated to a place knowing that it held plants and animals they depended upon. How did they know? Older members steered the band to reliable food sources based on their memory of past migrations. The Ute called these areas the Lower Earth (lowlands and canyons), the Middle Earth (mountain valleys and hills), and the Upper Earth (high ridges and peaks). Other aspects of Ute life and belief played a role in a band's migration.

Winter Camping

Cool air settled in valleys and made the lowlands very cold. So Utes built wickiups for the winter between 5,000 and 7,500 feet (1,500 and 2,300 m) up the mountains. Animals also moved into the same zone higher up to escape snow, giving the Ute game to hunt.

Hot Springs

Ute travelers used the many hot springs found in the Rockies for healing, relaxation, and religious ceremonies. Different Indian peoples or Ute bands often competed for the best springs.

Wise Use

The Ute, like most Native Americans, took only what they needed from the land. For that reason, game animals and useful plants did not die out. This guaranteed that more would be waiting when a Ute band returned to the same place the next year.

During the late winter, the Ute peeled ponderosa pine trees and ate the sweet inner bark.

Ute of all ages take part
in the Bear Dance.

CHAPTER 3

Ceremonies

The Ute had ceremonies that marked the change of seasons. Like many Plains peoples, they held a dance on the summer **solstice**. In the autumn, a ceremony took place before they began to harvest pine nuts. But the best-known Ute ceremony, and one of the most important, was the Bear Dance. It was devoted to the grizzly, the largest and most dangerous animal in the Rockies.

← The Bear Dance is the oldest Ute ceremony.

King of the Mountain

The grizzly is a type of brown bear. The male can rear up to stand 7 to 9 feet (2 to 3 m) tall and may weigh 600 to 1,000 pounds (270 to 450 kilograms). Over short distances, a grizzly can run 30 miles (50 kilometers) per hour—as fast as a horse. Grizzlies sleep during the winter. In March, the bears leave their dens. This is the same time the Ute moved out of their winter wickiups to find food.

The Ute believed grizzly bears had unusual powers.

Female grizzlies defend their young fiercely.

This created a dangerous situation. The female grizzlies were fierce because they were protecting their cubs. All the bears were hungry after the long winter. To add to the danger, Utes often met grizzlies when searching for berries, acorns, and meat—the same foods the bears ate. So to calm the grizzlies, the Ute gathered for the Bear Dance around the first day of spring.

The Bear Dance

According to one **tradition**, a grizzly bear taught the Bear Dance to a Ute hunter. The bear promised that as long as the Ute danced the Bear Dance, their hunters would find prey and their women would have many children. For hundreds of years, and on until today, the Ute have welcomed spring with this dance. Different bands gather to take part in the Bear Dance and to exchange news, celebrate spring, and have fun.

The Ute Bear Dance consists of a series of short dances.

Today's Bear Dances

Today, Ute Bear Dances often take place for four days in May. At the dance, women and men separate into two lines and dance back and forth for a time. Then the women choose male dance partners. Musicians continue to play the *morache*, an old Ute instrument that makes a noise like a growling bear. Dances today, like those in the past, draw Utes into a single community after a hard winter.

Women wear shawls over their shoulders during the Bear Dance. They flip their shawls in the men's faces, inviting them to dance.

In the 1800s, the Ute were placed on reservations such as this one in southwestern Colorado.

CHAPTER 4

Coming Back

Once they had been forced onto reservations, the Ute faced a long period of hard times. Promised supplies often failed to show up. Government officials insisted the Ute give up their style of clothing and even the way they wore their hair. The government also ordered the Ute to stop hunting and learn to farm. Mining companies and settlers, meanwhile, pushed to take over land on the Ute reservations.

By 1882, most of the Ute in Colorado had been removed from the state.

Land Problems

In 1905, President Theodore Roosevelt took more than 1 million acres (400,000 hectares) of land from the Uintah and Ouray Reservation in Utah to create a national forest. More land went to other projects and towns. Four years later, the reservation had shrunk from 4 million acres (1.6 million ha) to 360,000 acres (145,700 ha). Worse, Mormon settlers redirected the water Ute farmers needed to grow crops.

A Ute Timeline

1640
Utes begin trading for horses.

1865–1867
The Black Hawk War is fought against Mormon settlers.

The Low Point

No one knows how many Ute roamed the Rockies when the Spanish reached the area in the 1630s. But archaeologists think it was between 8,000 and 10,000 people. By the early 1900s, however, the Ute probably numbered fewer than 2,000. Their life of migration and hunting was mostly gone. Yet, the Ute survived the clash with white culture. By the 1930s, their numbers and lands began to increase again.

1930s
The Ute population rises.

1881
Utes are are forced onto reservations.

The Southern Ute

The Southern Ute live on a narrow reservation located in southwestern Colorado. They once had lost half their original land, but they began to get some back in the 1930s. The land would not work for farms. But as it turned out, valuable oil and natural gas existed underground, as did coal. These provided the Southern Ute with money. In recent years, the tribe has invested in high-tech companies and added jobs by building a casino.

Natural gas is a fuel that is used for many purposes, including cooking.

The Southern Ute Reservation sits atop one of the largest supplies of natural gas in the United States.

38

In the 1940s, the Ute attended a special hearing in an attempt to obtain payment for lands taken from them.

The Utah Utes

Even more land was taken from the Uintah and Ouray Reservation in Utah than from the Southern Ute Reservation. White ranchers took over some of the land the Ute used to feed livestock. **Poverty** was a serious problem. Even in the 1950s, most of the people on the reservation lacked water, electricity, and windows in their homes. But the U.S. government began to make changes that would slowly improve the situation.

UTE INDIAN MACHINE AND MANUFACTURING

About 3,000 Ute live on the Uintah and Ouray Reservation.

Manufacturing, or the production of goods, provides some jobs on the Uintah and Ouray Reservation.

Freedom and Profits

In the 20th century, the Ute gained the power to run their reservations as they wished. Councils of leaders replaced chiefs. The Ute took control of police forces, schools, and other services that the U.S. government had been managing.

The U.S. Congress, meanwhile, returned some of the Ute's lost land. The Ute bought more of it back. By the year 2010, the Uintah and Ouray Reservation had grown to more than 4.5 million acres (1.8 million ha). Oil and gas are mined on the reservation, and some Utes own businesses there.

Looking Ahead

Today, about 7,000 Ute live on three reservations: the Uintah and Ouray in Utah, the Southern Ute in Colorado, and the Ute Mountain Ute in southwestern Colorado. Ute live elsewhere, too. In fact, some Ute leaders worry that too many young people leave the reservations and ignore the Ute ways. To keep children linked to the Ute past, reservation schools offer lessons in the Ute culture and language.

Taking part in cultural events together is one way for Ute parents to pass traditions on to their children.

41

The Ute people still face hurdles. Many are poor. Diabetes is a major health problem. People can find it hard to get work. Getting back land taken in the past requires time and money.

There is good news, however. The Ute population is growing. Income from oil, natural gas, and coal have made the Southern Ute one of the wealthiest tribes in the United States. Like the grizzly after a hard winter, the Ute have awakened. ★

A Southern Ute boy participates in a traditional dance.

True Statistics

Number of Ute before contact with Spanish: 8,000 to 10,000

Ute population in the early 1900s: Fewer than 2,000

Number of Utes killed in the Black Hawk War: More than 50

Number of Ute language speakers today: More than 1,000

Size of the Uintah and Ouray Reservation today: 4.5 million acres (1.8 million ha)

Number of Ute reservations: 3

Number of Utes living on the reservations: About 7,000

The value of Southern Ute property and businesses today: About $2 billion

Total number of Utes living everywhere: 10,000

Grizzly bear

Did you find the truth?

(F) The Ute never rode on horseback.

(T) Ute dance the Bear Dance to honor the grizzly.

Resources

Books

Becker, Cynthia S. *Chipeta: Ute Peacemaker*. Palmer Lake, CO: Filter Press, 2008.

Doherty, Katherine M. *The Ute*. Vero Beach, FL: Rourke, 1994.

Gray-Kanatiiosh, Barbara A. *Ute*. Edina, MN: Checkerboard, 2004.

Kent, Deborah. *Utah*. Danbury, CT: Children's Press, 2009.

Krudwig, Vickie Leigh. *Searching for Chipeta*. Golden, CO: Fulcrum, 2004.

Lassieur, Allison. *The Utes*. Mankato, MN: Bridgestone, 2002.

Ryan, Marla Felkins, and Linda Schmittroth. *Ute*. Farmington Hills, MI: Blackbirch Press, 2003.

Organizations and Web Sites

The Ute Indian Tribe

www.utetribe.com
Read about the history of Utah's Ute, and find out what's going on today on the reservation.

Ute Mountain Ute Tribe

www.utemountainute.com
Click on links to learn about Ute history and legends and to see Ute pottery.

Places to Visit

Southern Ute Cultural Center & Museum

77 County Road 517
Ignacio, CO 81137
(970) 563-9583
www.succm.org
Explore the history and culture of the Southern Ute tribe at a new museum on the Southern Ute Reservation.

Ute Indian Museum

17253 Chipeta Drive
Montrose, CO 81401
(970) 249-3098
www.coloradohistory.org/hist_sites/UteIndian/Ute_indian.htm
Learn about Ute art and history at a museum located on the land of the Ute chief Ouray.

Important Words

archaeology (ar-kee-OL-uh-jee)—the study of past times and people through objects and remains of the past

breechcloths (BREECH-kloths)—pieces of clothing that hang down below the waist in the front and back

campaign (kam-PAYN)—a series of battles

drought (DROUT)—a long period of unusually low rainfall

hot springs (HOT SPRINGS)—springs or pools of water heated by volcanic activity

migrated (MY-grate-ed)—moved from one place to another

mobile (MOH-buhl)—able to move quickly and easily

moccasins (MOK-uh-suhnz)—soft heelless shoes or boots

poverty (POV-ver-tee)—a state of being poor

reservation (rez-ur-VAY-shuhnz)—land set aside for use by Native Americans

solstice (SOL-stis)—the first day of summer or winter

tradition (truh-DISH-uhn)—pattern of thought or action passed down from generation to generation

treaty (TREE-tee)—an agreement or deal that is legally binding on the two or more groups who sign

wickiup (WIK-ee-up)—a dome-shaped home with a wooden frame covered with bunches of brush or stiff grass

Index

Page numbers in **bold** indicate illustrations

About the Authors

Kevin Cunningham has written more than 40 books on disasters, the history of disease, Native Americans, and other topics. Cunningham lives near Chicago with his wife and young daughter.

Peter Benoit is educated as a mathematician but has many other interests. He has taught and tutored high school and college students for many years, mostly in math and science. He also runs summer workshops for writers and students of literature. Benoit has written more than 2,000 poems. His life has been one committed to learning. He lives in Greenwich, New York.